Mindful thoughts for
MOTHERS

First published in the UK and North America in 2019 by

Leaping Hare Press

An imprint of The Quarto Group, The Old Brewery,
16 Blundell Street, London N7 9BH, United Kingdom
T (0)20 7700 6700 **F** (0)20 7700 8066
www.QuartoKnows.com

British Library Cataloguing-in-Publication Data
A catalogue record for this book is available from the British Library

ISBN: 978-1-78240-765-2

This book was conceived, designed and produced by

Leaping Hare Press

58 West Street, Brighton BN1 2RA, UK

Publisher: *Susan Kelly*
Editorial Director: *Tom Kitch*
Art Director: *James Lawrence*
Commissioning Editor: *Monica Perdoni*
Project Editor: *Joanna Bentley*
Illustrator: *Lehel Kovacs*

Printed in China

1 3 5 7 9 10 8 6 4 2

Mindful thoughts for
MOTHERS

A journey of loving-awareness

Riga Forbes

Leaping Hare Press

Contents

Mindfulness in
Mothering

Motherhood is one of the most wonderful and powerful experiences we can have in life. Yet for a mother, being able to relax and find her flow in the busyness of the world today is an absolute necessity. To begin with, we can potentially go through a lot during pregnancy, childbirth and beyond, which is both physically and emotionally intense. Our reserves overall might become depleted, for a time at least, and we can feel destabilized by these factors. As the early years of our children's lives unfold, we will undoubtedly experience the heartfelt joys they bring, but will also encounter the stresses and demands that appear daily and nightly on the parenting path.

To manage these alongside the needs of our growing, dependent children, it is not enough for a mother to be just physically well; the task of mothering happy, relaxed children requires that we feel relaxed and happy too. Prioritizing our own enjoyment of life matters, and for the amazing and challenging task of mothering to be able to touch our hearts deeply, our lifestyle needs to support relaxation. Rest and exercise are vital, but slowing down our mental busyness will also enable us to become more conscious in how we meet the day to day.

Using mindfulness practice we can become quieter internally, helping us to release stress and to develop the discerning capacity to observe our thinking rather than simply being led by it. Gradually we can start to disengage from distracting thoughts by becoming more 'present' and meeting life with awareness, in the moment. This can also enable us to find greater self-understanding and to choose how we want to be, which will support our parenting and, in turn, positively influence who our children are becoming.

And at the heart of mothering lies the navigation of relationships within a family. If we can address issues that arise between us with a mindful approach, becoming more present and receptive in our interactions, we may find that we can steer our way through friction or difficulties towards open-heartedness. By being compassionate we offer our children a more generous perspective on relating to others, which will travel with them a long way and may well help them to overcome their own hurdles in life. Our love matters so much. And making more space for quiet reflection and meditation can help us to keep our hearts open. When we consider the countless benefits this practice brings into our lives and the lives of our families, it might seem like a nourishing kind of reward for all that we do.

I have written this book for every one of you who chooses to take a few moments – just for yourself – to curiously glimpse through these pages. May it support you to find the spaciousness, insight and self-kindness that you deserve.

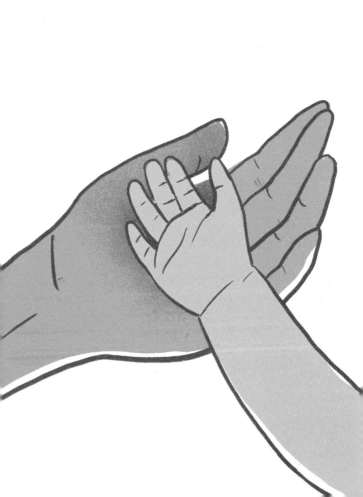

Love
– A Beginning Without End

From pregnancy on, we are forever linked to each of our children in some way, even as they grow older and live independently. And we will always be in their thoughts, feelings and memories too, even beyond our own lifespan. The power of the mother-child bond, initiated in pregnancy and childbirth, is a deep-seated instinctual force that quite simply causes us to care about each other. Our relationship may be rocky at times, but for a mother there is likely to be a taproot of love for her to draw on in times of drought, an overriding sense of connection to the child who came through her into this world.

THE CYCLE OF GIVING

In the beginning, when we were so entwined with our babies, this sense of connection may have been tangible as we smelt our child's skin or the milk on their breath. We might have felt it in the warmth of their small body wrapped up against our own as we fed them, or through gazing at their face. The relationship of nurture between a mother and her baby or toddler asks that a mother receives a generous helping of the reward, and that she too feels the benefit of this cycle of giving, even when she is doing the lion's share of it.

As we live through our children's younger years alongside them, in that elastic-time that can seem gradual and rapid in equal measure, our loving mother-child connection will find other experiences on which to anchor itself – sweet-funny child language and gestures, little rituals, games or interests that are unique to our child at that point in their lives, in which we participate. And when our children cross the bridge of maturity towards puberty and ultimately adulthood, this sense of connection may be more spacious, but at an unconscious level it will still be composed of their milky-breath smell and those funny words and the feel of their small hand in our own, because deep down we have known the whole picture from before their first breath, and we will always be able to feel it.

HEART-AND-MINDFULNESS

The mother-child bond is an amazing thing. Its power can make us protectors and champions of our children's rights, wellbeing and happiness. It can influence our own life choices as we prioritize our children, and it can inspire us to challenge whatever might threaten their prospects for a happy future. The energy of motherhood can make us powerful, and powerful we are. But not in an exploitative sense. Mother-energy embodies a life force that is heart-centred because ultimately it is born from the love we feel for our children.

The Buddhist Sanskrit word *citta* can be translated to mean both 'mind' and 'heart', and it encompasses both of these physical areas of the body along with their respective attributes of thought and feeling. But the term 'mindfulness' comes from the word *sati*, which means 'awareness' or 'remembering the truth of reality'. In the West, where we are so cerebral in our approach to life, our idea of mindfulness is often influenced by the misunderstanding that 'mind' means the brain. In fact, meditation engages citta, which is both brain and heart, and the awareness we encounter through regular practice may help us to observe our mental, emotional and physical states, but is ultimately seated in the heart. If it wasn't such a mouthful, I have often thought we should call meditation 'heart-and-mindfulness'.

MAKING SPACE FOR SELF-LOVE

'Heart-and-mindfulness' speaks to the compassion-focused core of the motherhood journey, too. We know compassion, we feel it deep inside, we hold it when we hold our child or think of them – not always, of course, but in essence. And compassion is an exceptionally beautiful thing. It is a healing force and it is so very much needed in the world right now. But it is even more potent when it comes from a place of authentic self-love in us, or from our intention to cultivate this.

As we travel along the path of motherhood, we might be conditioned by our intense early experiences of mothering, to focus on giving and providing love for others, yet we may forget to 'feel the love' ourselves too. This is not a self-indulgent notion, but one whose effects can be far-reaching and reflect into every aspect of our lives. The more space we can make to consciously receive kindness, joy and care, the more real and nourishing our cycle of maternal loving can be. Allowing more mindful moments of each day to become clear pools from which we can drink in the goodness life has to offer, could be the treasure our maternal hearts seek.

The First
Few Months

Nothing can really prepare us for becoming a mother
to a newborn baby, except perhaps living with or
supporting someone else who is doing just that. Even
then, we wouldn't experientially know what it is to be
recovering from childbirth, experiencing hormonal
changes and possibly learning to breastfeed while
adjusting to this new parental role. It is full-on and
most new parents' lives are quite literally turned upside
down by it. Night merges into day and day into night.
The jumbling effect of sleep deprivation can make us
feel spaced-out and utterly exhausted and can
compound the already heightened emotions of our
hormonal interior.

Although this period is at times an extreme and challenging phase, it is just that . . . a phase, which will soon become something different. Equally, the very beautiful bits of early motherhood – the falling in love, the closeness and discovery between parent and baby – are temporal states too, and will evolve soon enough into new forms and patterns. It can be powerful to bring a mindful outlook to the impermanence of those first few months of motherhood because, whether we like or dislike what is happening, unless we become present to it, it will pass us by.

LIVING IN THE PRESENT MOMENT

Many mothers say, 'The first few months are a total blur in my memory', and this can be even more so if sleep was especially scant or if they have one child or more already. Steering one's conscious awareness into the present moment may feel like one more thing on the 'to do' list, but if you can manage to make a few openings in the day or night just to focus on your bodily experience, your breathing, and then gradually on your immediate surroundings, bringing your full awareness into all that you sense, this can allow you to drop a little deeper into your engagement with the present.

Sometimes reminding ourselves to 'be here and now' can become a prompt to drop the worrying mind or the 'doing' trajectory and to shift into 'being' mode, offering ourselves an interval of rest at the same time. Many mothers would say that rest is a priority in the early months because they know that this is how we avoid burnout. We have a long journey ahead of us and our family really needs us to be well overall, so that each one of us can flourish.

RECEIVING AND GIVING

This phase in our lives is one in which we learn to truly appreciate someone making us a warm drink and other kinds of help and support that is given. We are grateful for every bit of sleep or nap we get, and in the delicate state we may be in we really feel the nourishment of good food. At moments when we can receive, it is good to pause and take it all in, to feel it, to be revived by it. In the same way, during the intimate times when we are feeding our babies, becoming conscious of our own giving, and tuning in to our little one receiving, will enable us to 'be' in this act with more awareness, and we will be much more likely to remember these precious times when they are long gone.

LOOKING INWARD AND REACHING OUT

On the flip side, we can bring in these tools to help us through the heavier states of early motherhood, such as the baby blues, postnatal depression or quite simply feeling low. Most women will experience some degree of this spectrum, and this can bring up feelings of disappointment, failure or shame that only compound our condition. If we can release our own judgements and other's expectations about how we 'should' be feeling and begin to accept and become curious about the feelings themselves, we may be able to understand more about our emotional responses to this intense time of life. Remembering that our hormones are very much in charge and our feelings are, in part at least, contrived by the complex chemical dance in our bodies in the months after birth, can help us to stop blaming ourselves if the going gets tough. And if it all gets too much, particularly if you think you might be suffering from postnatal depression, just reach out for some help – things can only get better if you do.

When we look back on this time and consider the levels of endurance needed to mother a tiny baby, it might seem like the most natural thing is to call on others, whether we are struggling or not. New parents and families need to feel supported, and when they are, everything feels easier.

Mothering
Together

As a mother, it is good to remember that at any given moment you are doing something that many, many other women are also doing, simultaneously – whether something momentous such as preparing to give birth, or something day-to-day such as changing a nappy, helping your child get dressed or setting boundaries for your unruly teenager. As individual women, the reality is that each of us is concurrently immersed in a wider network of common experience, and living with an awareness of this can feel very reassuring.

But it is even more helpful to make physical space and time in our lives to meet and talk together, to cry and laugh about the extremes and edges of what we go through both practically and internally as mothers. This process of sharing and empathizing with other mothers enables us to grow so much. We can share issues that are relevant to our collective experience. This gives us the chance to release accumulated stresses, to gain insight, perspective and support in ways that can help us to feel we are not alone with it all. We can be nourished, our strength renewed and our load lightened.

A POTENTIALLY LONELY PATH

As a new mother there were so many times when I felt out of my depth with the weight of responsibility I was carrying – not entirely because of that weight in itself, but because often I felt isolated with it. The effort it can take to do whatever is needed for ourselves and our baby while maintaining a social agenda of meetups and groups, being organized, getting in and out of buses or cars, all while sleep deprived, is just too much for some of us. I found it easier to make my life as simple as possible, but sometimes this meant not spending enough time with other mothers or adults. Early motherhood can feel like a lonely experience without regular contact with women who share the maternal experience, and the lack of this is statistically shown to contribute to postnatal depression and anxiety.

I do not believe that we were meant to raise children alone. Feeling our common ground and kinship with others is a core part of feeling supported and connected as a parent, and this hugely contributes to our happiness on every level.

SHARING THE LOAD

There is a saying, 'It takes a village to raise a child'. For me, this notion stems from our shared history as a species: we have originated from tribal groups where children were raised by the entire community, and not by their blood parents alone. The outcome of communal parenting in this way can bring many positive elements into the lives of both adults and children. A child can learn and grow up with a more rounded understanding of the world he or she lives in, and parents can raise their children without feeling as if they are running the show with no back-up.

Engaging with like-minded communities can really uplift us as families. It can soften the edges of our sole responsibility as parents and it can expand our children's horizons beyond the nuclear family, building trust, compassion and interdependence along the way. This village approach can be related to the word *sangha* in Buddhism, which signifies a spiritual community. Originally this term referred to a group of monks or nuns living and practising together, but as a theme it can also be viewed more widely as a gathering of non-secular groups who have a collective focus to support each individual as well as the group as a whole.

AN INTERCONNECTED WEB

However, we don't have to live communally to feel connected in this way. A sangha can be forged within our close family and friendship circles and today even among social-media groups. It may be strengthened by reading the ideas of others, and through the study and practice of things we feel passionate about. Rather than occupying a physical, peopled space, it can be composed of a sense of connection within us.

As mothers we can attune to this feeling of interconnectedness, our shared link through the acts of giving birth and nurturing, and in some way feel part of a sangha of women. We have more in common than we might realize: a shared experience of the physical stages of womanhood, and a mutual hope for the flourishing of our children and for the generations yet to come. And as we recognize our many bonds, across the distinctions of nation, culture and race, we may feel increasingly more aligned with each other.

Identity
– Self, Mother and Consciousness

Having crossed the portal of birth, do you remember the first moment you began to catch up with yourself, and found that you were a foreigner to the memory of your life before children? Or perhaps a stranger to your new life as a mother? I think that most mothers will at some point reflect on this contrast in their life experience, perhaps asking themselves the question, 'who was I then?' followed by 'and who am I now?' I adore my children, and yet there will always be a kind of gazing back to the life I lived up until they arrived, with a sense of awe for all the freedom that I hadn't even known was mine.

This contrast between then and now might be particularly acute if a woman's life before children involved a high degree of independence, intellectual focus, perhaps travel or having to look 'presentable'. Suddenly, looking neat in public becomes a little less realistic, our intellect is underchallenged yet derailed by hormones and lack of sleep, a lifestyle that was once lively and varied starts to border on being repetitive and home-bound. And the overall focus in life shifts from worldly achievement to filling little bellies and avoiding bottom rashes.

IN PRAISE OF MOTHERHOOD

In the eyes of society, being a career woman is rated more highly than raising the next generation of human beings on this planet. And society's eyes do bring a quality of judgement upon what we do. While many mothers love their careers and will rightly do whatever possible to maintain them as they raise their young, those who prioritize childrearing and forgo earning a salary might feel that their vocation is somehow less valued. So often I have heard myself or other mothers speaking with guilt or frustration the words, 'Oh, I haven't managed to do anything today', when in reality we have masterfully fed, cared for and responded to the needs of our children and ourselves. We might have successfully diffused conflict, managed to stay calm in the face of adversity, synchronized our offspring's naps and developed creative listening skills all in the space of 12 hours or less. But we see it as nothing because it is 'just' childcare.

The more mindful we become of this self-diminishing attitude, the easier it is to charge ourselves with the task of cultivating pride in our unpaid, skilled work as mothers, knowing that what we bring to the world matters. A child who is well cared for will contribute to humanity from a resource of inner wealth which cannot be compared to material wealth. It is a profound responsibility we hold and it needs to be seen apart from career and finances.

The psychological leap into motherhood is huge, and its significance is largely overlooked in modernized societies. So often women come to be mothers without any clear cultural confirmation or acknowledgement of the process being such a major life transition. Traditional peoples have other ways of honouring this personal evolution in a woman's life, such as the Navajo tribal 'Hozhooji', or 'Blessingway', a community ceremony that celebrates and nurtures a mother in late pregnancy, blessing the birth of her new baby to come.

Being honoured and celebrated in this way can make our progression through motherhood more meaningful, while helping to reduce feelings of isolation. It can aid the integration of our new identity and gift us with the strength and self-esteem needed for the journey ahead. Beyond this, perhaps it can also help us to connect with the spiritual side of ourselves, bringing more depth and meaning to all we do. It can be reassuring for a mother to feel that she belongs to a supportive community who are there for her.

OUR ESSENTIAL SELF

There is an astute analogy about the continuous 'presence' of our consciousness being like the single thread on which the many varied beads of our life experience are strung. The beads of childhood may be very distinct from those of adulthood, yet the fibre at the core of our being is a constant throughout. We can witness ourselves as transitional beings, our lives a metamorphosis through phase after phase, from our own birth onwards. Our 'identity' embodies a personalized aspect of ourselves at any given time of our lives. Motherhood is just one part of our life experience but the essence of who we are is unchanging.

Spiritual teacher Ram Dass portrays this idea of the true self in his mantra, 'I am loving awareness'. Beyond all else, the mantra states, way beyond all our personal stories, this awareness is what we are. And in meditation we might notice that the ongoing narrative of our many-layered identity begins to slip, veil by veil, revealing just this bright conscious awareness, now.

Threads of
Connection

There is a Buddhist meditation practice called *Metta bhavana*, or 'Loving-kindness Meditation', which guides us to open our heart, firstly towards ourselves, and then to others: those close to us, those we hardly know, and then those in our wider community and beyond. Gradually our positive, supportive feelings are generated and extended out to all sentient beings. The *Metta* practice is metaphorically like planting a seed of love within ourselves, one that continues to grow and expand outward. In this way it can be seen to echo the essence of mothering, which also plants a seed of love that will develop through the process of gestating and nurturing a child.

We grow together through the years, changing yet unchanging, at some level always mother and always child. But this bond of ours is also woven into our extended families and inner circles, playgroups, schools, and steadily out into the wider web of our communities. These loving threads of connection between us can continue to extend in other ways through us, throughout our lives, as we continue to connect with others.

SEEING THROUGH ANOTHER'S EYES

Since becoming a mother, my sense of compassion and connection with families has intensified as I find my own life reflected in the lives and stories of others. I have more understanding now because I have been there and I can relate to another from this insider's perspective. In the grand scheme of things, having children is an act that enables more empathy between us. Human beings, and creatures too, cannot help but be somehow living in relationship with one another, as we co-exist together, in this very moment.

The Dalai Lama often speaks about the wish for happiness that all living beings share. This is our common personal goal, and so many of the things we do from day to day in our lives have this intention behind them, even if they might seem quite unrelated. Becoming aware of our collective desire for happiness enables us to perhaps see a little more through the eyes of another. We can understand, for example, that if anger or fear arise in someone, this may be because a protective instinct has been triggered, which is an expression of a personal wish to be safe and therefore, at some level, a desire to maintain happiness.

Seeing this drive towards happiness as not just a personal but also a shared intent, can help us to identify with, rather than feel alienated by, someone whose behaviour may be very different from our own. This is not always easy, and it may require us to explore a person's backstory to really be able to see things from their perspective, but it is a brave step in the direction of generating more compassion in the way we see others.

WE ARE ALL DAUGHTERS AND SONS

From certain Native North American tribal traditions there comes a wise saying that encompasses the very essence of compassionate thinking, 'I am another one of yourself'. For me, this idea comes closest to our motherly experience of birthing and bonding with our babies. Taking part in this miracle of life-creation, witnessing another body emerging from our own, feeding our babies skin-to-skin . . . these are the most heightened and visceral moments we will ever experience in our connectedness as human beings.

Knowing that all of us are daughters or sons and have been born to a mother reinforces this sense of human connectedness. Any mother who has adopted a baby or child will know it, and deep down we all have the potential to recognize that while we may be 'separate' in body, we are related through our hearts. Physically we are individual, yet there is no separation when we perceive life from the angle that everyone and everything is living energy or life force. It and we are all simply alive.

CULTIVATING KINDNESS

Our connectedness as human beings can be directly experienced if we focus our meditation on compassion. But in the day to day, cultivating kindness doesn't always feel easy. It can be humbling to spot how many times we might fumble through an interaction with someone, intent on getting a task done successfully rather that bringing our open hearts to the fore, making eye contact and wishing them well as we go on our way. Making the effort to keep developing kindness towards all beings is a life-long undertaking. It is helpful to remember, though, how powerful it can be to show your care for the wellbeing of those you meet.

Through us, the influence of kindness can spread its ripples wider, touching the lives of our children, families and communities, and helping to bring this simple attitude of care into the wider world. Take a moment to breathe and feel your connection to all life. Send some love to yourself and to all those around you.

The Imperfect Mother

Show me a 'perfect mother' and I will show you a 'perfect child' ... but we may have to look very hard to find either of them because the truth is they just don't exist. So where does this notion that we should aim for perfection originate from and why does it play heavily on the hearts of so many of us? Maternal guilt can uproot us from the very ground on which we stand. It can create negative thought cycles in our minds, self-doubt and heartache. Just how perfect do we have to be to avoid it?

In order to understand the perfect-mother archetype it is helpful to cast our minds back to the time frame during which it was constructed. Throughout history women have generally been defined as either mother or unmarried maiden. Over the course of recent millennia, generations of women have fulfilled and identified with a role that was both characterized and judged by the socio-religious setting in which they lived. Mothers were encouraged to embody the traits of obedient wife and dutiful care-provider, as exemplified by archetypal figures from the religious stories and scriptures of their given culture. The fulfilment of these requirements, for the most part, became the social law underpinning a mother's life-purpose.

Because we are only just now starting to shift away from the patriarchal systems that have instilled these attitudes into us for so long, a woman's vocational scope in life has until relatively recent times been hugely limited and controlled. And in some contexts it still is. Traditionally, when we became mothers it was guaranteed that all eyes would be upon us to ensure we performed the role well enough. In a generic sense, this pressure to meet the mark has made its way intently down through the ages into our collective consciousness, via glossy magazine images that play on our insecurities, and into the psyches of women who are mothering today. It has blended seamlessly with our natural longing for our children to be happy and well, and consequently it can be a confusing and preoccupying theme.

THE MYTH OF THE PERFECT MOTHER

We readily fall into guilt-tripping thoughts like, 'If only I had/could/did/didn't . . .' or, 'What did I do wrong?' with regard to our children's welfare. Turning a mindful and objective eye to these thoughts, we can observe that our wishes to achieve the very best outcomes for our children are overlaid by ancestral expectations about excelling as a mother. We have inherited a legacy of guilt. We hold so much responsibility and sometimes we have to make difficult choices. Every choice we make has a consequence and inevitably sometimes mistakes are made. But by trying our best and being authentic, we teach our children that they can do this too.

When we are confronted by our own idea of a perfect mother, either incarnate or imagined, we might compare ourselves to this and start up the inward cycle of thoughts that tells us we are inadequate. However, we can also draw on mindfulness skills, which enable us to become present and to see judgements like this as an obscuration of reality. Every mother and child are unique, as is every parent-child relationship. As mothers we can always try to improve on bits of us that need work, but perhaps we also need to recognize that being who we truly are is good enough and perfect in its own way.

BE TRUE TO YOURSELF

If we can learn to let go of our ideas of perfection and instead turn to face what 'is', we may feel more empowered to respond to the real needs of our children and ourselves, rather than trying to be someone's idea of 'perfect'. We have all experienced mothering of some kind, whether from an actual mother, a mother figure, friend or foster mother. We know it is a human gift of love and it will always have its odd angles and edges.

If we can make peace with this, recognizing the value of our humanness and authenticity as we mother, accepting when we fall down and when we excel, the easier our path can be, for both ourselves and our children. Cultural ideals and standards that define how we ought to look or be, or our own internalized versions of these, only generate feelings of unworthiness. It takes courage to show up just as we are, but if we do, we can model this empowering strength for our children, and perhaps they can do the same for theirs. Most importantly we can consciously learn how to accept and truly be ourselves, which is perhaps the greatest gift of all.

Tantrums

Tantrums: we all have them from time to time, let's not pretend. And sometimes a family can be like a trail of dominoes where one member's tantrum triggers another's, and then another's. Yet the toddler tantrum can reach epic proportions way beyond the scale of any Wagner opera or heavy metal performance known to humankind, as I bore witness to when my son was of that age. This is one of the drawbacks to parenting little ones that we simply have to learn to accept and be with, as and when it arises. Among all the parenting manuals I have read, I have never come across any advice that could offer an effective counter-response to tantrums, other than . . . breathe.

TAKING TIME TO BREATHE

And actually, breathing does work. If we turn our total attention to our breath, this stops us from following the impulse to run away or to reach for an imaginary 'off' button. Instead, we return our focus back to ourselves – in the here-and-now – and to the simple passage of our breath in and out of our body, letting it soften some of the tension we may have been holding. Already the tantrum our child is engaged in feels slightly less centre stage as we begin to relax with it.

But what if, for example, our fuse gets lit by the inferno our child is generating and we react with anger ourselves? This situation can be highly flammable and requires a more directed kind of conscious breathing. I suggest momentarily pausing and checking where you are feeling anger in your body. When you have located it, start to breathe into this area of your body, bringing your full conscious awareness to your physical experience. Stay there for as long as you can, just breathing with acceptance into the 'angry' part. If you do this for long enough, you will undoubtedly notice that something shifts. The tension begins to subside and breathing eases.

There is an age-old Buddhist adage that says, 'This too will pass', and it is good to try and remember this when your child is in the throes of protesting. One thing that is guaranteed in this lifetime is change. When a toddler's tantrum changes into something calmer, a parent is relieved, and when a child grows out of their tantrums altogether, a parent rejoices (until they become a teenager, at least). The important point is that change does happen eventually.

GOING WITH THE FLOW

Alongside our efforts to become present to our breath and body sensations, it is good for us to try to recognize that children and adults alike are entitled to blow their tops from time to time, so long as no one else gets hurt in the process. If we take a step back we can see that physiologically our toddlers are coping with lots of growth hormones in their systems and at times they are on a sleep deficit, which is likely to make anyone bad-tempered. There might also be things in the family environment that they pick up on unconsciously. On top of this, they have a limited lexicon for clearly understanding or verbally communicating their needs, and very little actual control over their lives. It makes sense that these circumstances may add to their feelings of frustration, culminating periodically in rage.

If we can let go of our train of thought about why they 'should not' be exploding or about how inconvenient or perhaps embarrassing it is, and just allow them to get on with it, they will eventually relax when they have finished. Obviously this might be easier to do at home than in the supermarket, where we may feel we are fully on show, but for the most part letting our children follow the natural course of their tantrums helps them, in turn, to ultimately find more acceptance for themselves and for life too. It is when we try to stop the flow that we bump into problems.

Although it might feel very uncomfortable to start with, the practice of simply giving space for our children to let off steam ultimately makes life a lot easier for us too. Although every parent wants a happy child, the reality is that if we negate or stifle our children's tempers at this early, formative stage in their development, we will be disempowering them later on with feelings of shame or wrongness around expressing their anger. If we can accept them when they are expressing all their emotional discomfort, imagine how much easier it will be for them to like themselves authentically in future life. Try thinking of it as an investment in their personal growth. Keep your sense of humour afloat – and don't forget to breathe!

Impermanence

When we become mothers, we are set on a path of learning about impermanence. Initially we must let go of our pre-mother body as we get to know and experience pregnancy. Then we surrender up this pregnancy to childbirth and all that it brings. Suddenly we become mothers, held in an intense and perpetual relationship with our newborn. But before we know it, our newborn metamorphoses into our toddler, our child, our teenager, and our adult son or daughter, and all the while life keeps asking us to open up and to let go into these tides of change. We have no alternative but to meet life as it comes - because time doesn't wait around for anyone.

The challenge is that sometimes we get stuck. Some part of us might not be willing to lose the baby that is now a tottering toddler or the child that has become our teen. We develop strong attachments to the past, to our remaining memories, and this can be a painful state. I know because I have experienced it often and I believe many women experience grief at times while witnessing their children growing up. The last days of breastfeeding, the emergence of a toddler's independence, the youngest child starting or leaving school. Landmarks such as these can pull at our maternal sense of loss, of this childhood phase ending forever.

LEARNING TO LET GO

I remember knowing I'd never be pregnant again after my youngest was born. When he was five we moved house and I came across a bag of the very special baby clothes I had saved as my children outgrew them. As I opened it and saw the moth-eaten remains of hand-knitted jumpers and little leather slippers, I was hit with an involuntary tidal wave of sadness and weeping, like a shock wave running through me. My rational mind did not have a chance to explain it away, as these feelings absolutely had to be expressed. When I had finished grieving, I put everything away and got on with my day, feeling lighter but moved in the wake of what had happened.

This kind of experience shouldn't be diminished as a spate of nostalgia or a sentimental outburst, but seen as a natural part of processing the powerful emotions that can underpin our relationship to our ever-changing children. We need these moments of letting go because we are constantly having to catch up with the next chapter of our child, and the next, and the next.

At such moments our best recourse is just to be with our feelings as they are, without suppressing or judging them, to check our breath and to follow its flow, to become aware of the sensations in our body and to bring ourselves back into the present moment in all its fullness. Coming back into the body when we have been experiencing psychological or emotional intensity is not always easy to do, but it is an effective way of re-centring ourselves. And when we come back to our centre, then we can begin to witness our experience with some kindness for ourselves.

MOVING FORWARD

Life involves pain, and pain comes and goes. It is a fact of life that we need to develop compassion for. We all suffer sometimes and it can be tough, really tough. If we learn to open our hearts to the pain we feel or to the pain felt by others, not only are we meeting it with acceptance, but we are also creating more care and nurturing, which is something that we all deeply need. This can take courage but the positive impact of welcoming feelings, rather than avoiding them, is huge.

If we find we are struggling with the swift evolution of our children into teens and adults it can also be helpful to take stock of all the benefits brought by this change. Their burgeoning independence makes our lives and workload so much easier. Feeling needed less can mean that we may feel freer, too. And as we watch our children metamorphosing ever onwards and upwards, we have the privilege of seeing them become fully grown individuals in their own right, who can hopefully help us out when we need them to, which is a blessing for any parent. The fact is that we are on a course set to learn that change is simultaneously sudden, gradual, and ultimately inevitable. And acknowledging this can help us to keep up with the new person our son or daughter is constantly becoming, and to adjust in ways that enable us to celebrate and go with it.

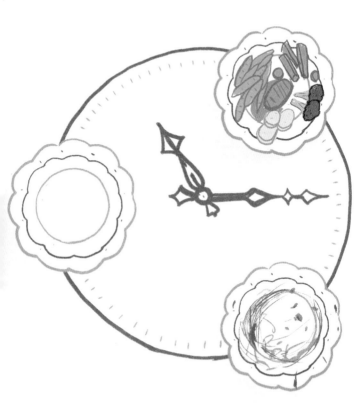

The Daily
Grind

Early on in our children's lives, we are needed 24/7. There is no replacement for a mother and we feature large in the centre of our children's world view. The truth is though, that alongside us, what our little ones also need is a sense of rhythm that they can get to know and relax into, based around two very important aspects of life: food and sleep. These rhythms will certainly change as they grow, but for the short term, we mothers are focused on meeting our children's needs within the scope of their current daily or nightly patterns.

The only glitch in this picture of routine, which is programmed to repeat over and over, is that our inner free spirit may feel very much excluded. The younger self, that pre-mother wild thing who used to stay out late and eat a bowl of cereal for dinner in the early hours of the morning? She may feel a little like she's been ditched in favour of keeping the children in a rhythmic continuity of being well fed and rested – a continuum that goes on for years.

MONOTONY AND MINDFULNESS

It may sound obvious, but repetition can become a deeply boring theme in motherhood until our children are grown up enough to cook, clean and conduct their own lives independently. Even if parental roles are shared or the father or partner is the primary carer, there will still be regular cadences in the melody of family life that can feel laboured and dull. The never-ending washing-up, the tidying toys away, the serving up of dinner by six o'clock or blood-sugar levels drop and mutiny ensues. This side of parenting might leave us yearning for freedom and we may just 'get through' these situations as if on autopilot.

But by bringing a mindful approach to well-worn patterns of activity, we call ourselves to 'wake up' during an unconscious act of 'doing' by becoming more aware. If we have very young children, they can help us here by teaching us how to see through fresh eyes. Their experience of what surrounds them makes a different kind of sense to the cognitive processes of an adult mind, partly because they have the inspiring ability to be 'in the moment'.

SEEING LIKE A CHILD

In her wonderful book *Drawing on the Right Side of the Brain*, art expert Betty Edwards suggests that as we grow up we learn to label the physical world around us and as soon as we have a word for an object we forget to experience it as it is, or in the way that a young child might. But if we get curious with our vision, a stick becomes so much more than a generic stick; it unfolds before the eye as a series of layers in dry or damp wood, textured, pitted, scarred, and softened in places, tonally distinct between the heartwood and the bark. An artist or photographer will find visual terms for a stick that the word 'stick' could never encompass.

Losing this immediacy of perception as we get older is all part of embedding the unconscious mind so that our conscious experience of our everyday environment doesn't leave us overwhelmed. The more familiar we are with our daily sphere of existence, the more we perceive what is around us at an unconscious level. But mindfulness practice can be one way of reclaiming our original capacity to be consciously immersed in the moment; to find ways of experiencing life without projecting, anticipating or assuming what we perceive.

This is a key tenet of Buddhism, where practitioners hold the intention to 'wake up' or experience an enlightened state of being. Meditation practice develops our ability to see everything with openness and clarity, free from judgements and overthinking, and in this way it helps us to generate some of the original curiosity and simplicity of seeing that we once knew as children.

A NEW WAKEFULNESS

Parents are usually having to cover a lot of bases just to keep everyone safe, fed and well and it might not seem like there is much opportunity to drop the carer role to run into the realms of innocence. But if we try to pause for a few minutes before attempting that tedious chore – and let our thoughts pass by, breath by breath, as we get really present in our body – we might start to notice a new wakefulness in among the humdrum. We can use our vision, hearing and all of our senses to open up into our experience. We can become aware of our feelings and sensations, and with practice we can begin to feel more alive in these monotonous windows of activity than we may ever have thought possible.

A Mother's
Radar

Little else equals the enormity of holding our first newborn babe. It is the grand introduction to our new role as a sustainer and protector of life and in the midst of it we may begin to consider the imminent reality that we will need to do everything possible to keep this little person alive and well. Alongside everything else we may be feeling post-birth, including the love, there may be a sense of fear surrounding this assignment, probably the most important responsibility of our life. And without doubt this first phase of our child's life primes us for the years ahead as we naturally become hormonally and emotionally aligned with ensuring their wellbeing and survival.

I call this 'sense' of ours a mother's radar. It signals to us when our child is distressed, hungry, tired, in danger or in need. When messages are firing we may feel discomfort, worry and even suffering until the hunger has been abated or safety has been restored. Looking at the bigger view, evolutionarily these sensitive mother-radars of ours actually ensure the wellness and survival of humankind. They are not to be underestimated.

Yet constantly living in the 'alert' zone can be very stressful. I remember being so flooded with adrenalin at times that my whole nervous system was knocked off kilter, affecting my sleep and energy levels. Above all else, I frequently felt tense. Perhaps some radars are more delicate than others, but the more times we are woken at night and the more 'incidents' we have to cope with during the day, the more wired we can become, and an overstimulated nervous system is not sustainable for optimum good health. It can make a dent on our wellness longer term and it can also contribute to breakdowns in parental relationships.

A HELPING HAND

If we want to protect this time of life for the sake of our children as well as ourselves, we must consider how to make life less demanding both during pregnancy and in the years that follow. It is so important for new families to realize that the first few years of any child's life is going to be intense for parents, and for us to try and engage every available support system we possibly can during those years. Because it will get easier, but early on you will enjoy the ride so much more if you have help with it. Ask your family and friends for assistance and accept help when it is offered. Make small but significant adjustments to your life that allow for quality downtime so that you can adopt healthy rhythms in your parenting, if possible.

TUNE IN TO YOUR INTUITION

If the alarm system on your maternal radar has been activated more times than is manageable and you are experiencing anxiety or a feeling of overwhelm because of this, see if you can address it by doing whatever helps you to combat stress and improve sleep. Try to heal the agitation in your system by prioritizing time to rest.

Our inner radars are vital and amazing, but even so it is good to keep checking in to see if the anxieties we have for our children are in proportion. Notice if they are realistic or whether they are stemming from our own perhaps unconsciously projected fears, for example recurring fears or worries about our child being hurt or rejected. Themes from our own childhood are often triggered by our children's experiences or our worries about what they could experience. Observe the spectrum of your impulses towards your offspring, ranging from curiosity to angst, and notice the ease or tension you may be holding around their safety. If you find that your energy is leaking away over certain needless fears, it is very valuable to explore ways of releasing them. The simplest way to start this is with eyes closed, breathing into any area of tension in your body and trying to soften and release anxiety on your out-breath.

Managing what we need to manage from day to day is made much harder by holding a weight of tension that stems from the roots of 'what if?' If we use this energy instead to attune to our natural intuition about our children, we may be amazed to find how much we are worrying less and yet are more aware. In many ways modern life has eroded our human intuitive faculties through coaxing us into dependency on information, gadgets and machines. We really have to get quiet enough to sharpen our inner knowing, but a mother's radar will give the clearest sense of recognition when she is relaxed and well in herself.

Challenges and
Acceptance

Life can be challenging for everyone at times, but there are some phases that top the rest, such as when we are parenting intensively during the first five years and feel as if life seems to pose a relentless string of demands. We may have an overriding sense of wanting to make our children happy, but feel that we are just about treading water while constantly steering through whatever challenges come up, from illness, teething and sleep deprivation to placating the strong wills of small children. Set this in the context of a modern world with work, shopping, traffic, paying of bills and meeting daily schedules, and we have all the ingredients for cumulative stress.

Sometimes we may feel like we want to parent with more awareness but we are being swept along with the tide and can't even think about where to begin. However, one step towards slowing down and becoming more conscious in the way we live, is to cultivate acceptance. By this I mean actively starting to recognize the challenges that are an intrinsic part of our lives, and finding a calm reference point within ourselves to acknowledge and accept them.

THE MIDDLE WAY

One of the teachings central to Buddhism is the 'Middle Path' or the 'Middle Way'. As a concept this can be read specifically in reference to the practices of monastic life, but it can also be interpreted more loosely as a general lifestyle choice that anyone can make. The Middle Way is the principle of accepting that everything in existence is dualistic: light and dark, night and day, life and death. It looks at the manifest world as a complex relationship of cause and effect, and it concludes that amid these often extreme conditions our wisest response is to be centred, remaining as unbuffeted as possible by life's ongoing tempest. As Buddhist author and teacher Jack Kornfield wrote in his book *The Wise Heart*, 'The more we delve into the middle way the more deeply we come to rest between the play of opposites.'

I see following the Middle Way as an inward journey that does not prevent us from taking a stand in life, fighting a cause or changing things that aren't working. On the contrary, taking this route can enable us to feel freer emotionally, so that creating change is naturally easier. Unless we can first find acceptance for any difficult situation, whether that be sleepless nights, sibling rivalry or something else entirely, we will be struggling against it and this will disempower us more than if we meet it face-on, as it is, unrestricted by inner conflict. To make positive change in life we will go further if we can calmly look into the eyes of adversity and then embody the positivity we seek to create.

BREATHE YOURSELF CALM

Creating peace in ourselves is not easy when the going gets tough, however. We can easily slip into well-worn patterns of reaction, such as anger, guilt or blame. We might explode under pressure and then regret our outbursts later. Being aware of our body tension and focusing on our breath can help to diffuse difficult feelings. One effective aid in tense situations when anger or irritation arises is a 'countdown' method of centring oneself with mindful breathing. This involves counting a number of slow, deep, conscious breaths, say three to five, before responding to whatever is happening around you, thereby allowing yourself a mindful moment in which to become calmer.

LEARNING FROM OUR CHILDREN

Our children often show a lot of courage when it comes to facing trials and adversities. So much of early life includes learning how to be in the world as an individual. Every day our young ones fail and succeed in different areas and activities and they keep on going, they keep trying even if things didn't work out the day before. We can take inspiration from them by trying to remain open to life and remember that we are still learning too and it's okay to fall down and get back up again. It is okay not to achieve our goals, or to redirect our efforts in some other way. Things that might initially confront or scare us could, somewhere further down the line, prove to be old hat.

As mothers we can be the rock in our children's lives, but it will help us if firstly we can practise being that rock ourselves. This means finding the place inside where we become the eye of the storm, and trusting it. The human psyche is a playground of opposites. If we can find stillness and acceptance there, then we can begin to find it in the world around us, faced with all its diverse experiences and impressions.

Gratitude

In our material world of today, living with an 'attitude of gratitude' can generate a different kind of mindset to that of our consumer culture, which perpetually encourages us to be greedy, to have more, to get more and to attain more. The advertising surrounding us in every form yells loudly at us to look to the new and discard anything outdated, even if it still works. Without wanting to diminish our aspiration for development and abundance, which are natural human desires, the outcome of this message can implant the idea in our minds that what we have and who we are is never enough. But if we muster the courage to momentarily step off this treadmill of 'want' generated by the avaricious ethos of our times, and start reflecting on our lives, just as they are, we may notice where we have lost sight of our appreciation.

A mother who has experienced the safe birth of her baby will know both gratitude for her child's life and for her own. A mother who has experienced the loss of a child may deeply know the preciousness of life through her grief. We mothers understand something about life's miraculous gift that is unique to ourselves. Touching upon intense and perhaps fragile places during childbirth and throughout childrearing can enable us to see clearly what is important to us. The special people in our lives take pride of place in our hearts and for their presence we feel grateful.

TAKING TIME TO BE GLAD

But when intensity fades out and normality fades in, as is the way in life, we may find that we have taken ourselves and others for granted. We may feel dissatisfaction with things as they are, and we may forget the profound thanksgiving for life itself that we had grasped before. This is normal; it is part of the cycle of forgetting and remembering life's sacredness, which enables us to develop wisdom. But it is also somehow heart breaking. Sitting in meditation has afforded me glimpses of insight into my own lack of appreciation at times, and this has motivated me to make changes in the way I see my life. The practice of gratitude can help us to turn things around. It is one of those interesting feelings that increases with application, and it falls gracefully into place with mindfulness in every way.

When we make use of a stray moment that might otherwise be gathered up into doing 'stuff', to simply take note of all the riches of our current experience, of all the things we are glad for, we may feel a lift in our heart. This might be an instant just long enough to reflect on one thing, for example, the sound of our children playing and laughing. But we can also make intervals here and there for dwelling more deeply on how grateful we are for our children and families; for the clean water and food we are able to share with them; for the useful or beautiful material things that we are able to surround ourselves and our families with; for the safety and freedom of each one of us; and for the feeling of community we can encounter both among strangers and close friends alike.

BREATHING IN AND LOOKING OUT

By focusing on our breathing in meditation we can hone our sense of gratitude for the very air that sustains us, and further still, for the erudite physiology within us that uses this air to give us all life. The more deeply we venture into the vivid workings of our physical bodies, the more miraculous they appear. We may realize quite how blessed we are to be living at all.

And when we turn our awareness outwards to what surrounds us – the buildings, the natural world, the sky, the living beings that we share this planet with – we might find ourselves in awe of the magnitude of these civilizations and ecosystems, people and creatures whose ever-changing networks of life continue to evolve and spiral, dying and rebirthing over seasons and aeons. For a mother, the fascinating experience of witnessing her baby growing up might bring equal wonder and gratitude at times. Landmark events such as birthdays can bring home a heartfelt sense of achievement, perhaps an intimate remembrance of our child's very first day of birth.

If you find yourself immersed in the familial swamp of things to do and small people's needs to attend to, feeling overloaded by it all, try closing your eyes, putting your hand on your heart and breathing calmly while bringing to mind the smiling faces of your children. Allow that glow of gratitude to arise in you if you can. Because feeling grateful benefits and connects all of us.

Adoration
and Irritation

'I can't live with him and I can't live without him!' my grandmother used to say in jest, referring to my father as a maverick little boy. For me this summarizes the parental dilemma we sometimes face, a fluctuating dynamic of love and loathing, like and dislike that can feel very real for us in relationship to our children.

Let's first contextualize this: it is not just that our children or their activities occasionally annoy us, but we may find them infinitely more annoying than usual because we are pre menstrual, or because we slept badly, or because we have low blood sugar after having gone without a proper breakfast, and so on. Being at a low ebb in ourselves inevitably influences our chances of 'keeping it together' when it comes to our children doing their own special irritating thing. Remembering to take care of our own needs is likely to avoid major maternal eruptions, which in the long run will serve us better all round. It goes without saying that mothers need to eat, rest and be well so that those sometimes-frayed nerve endings of ours have less to contend with around our children.

FINDING THE CENTRE GROUND

The quandary of like and dislike, or craving and aversion, has been the subject of Buddhist teachings for many centuries. This is primarily because it is an experience that is characteristic to all living things, but it is also because in order to become conscious of our thought patterns we need to consider what pulls at them and sways them in a particular direction and why. For example, the love we have for our children when they are calm and affectionate may cause us to react just as strongly against them when they are squabbling or demanding, because our yearning for the good times is not only unmet, but in this situation is taken to its opposite extreme of deprivation.

Here, the Buddhist principle of the Middle Way teaches that 'wanting' and 'not wanting' will lead us into a merry dance of opposites, and the only way to avoid getting sucked into this polarity is to find some semblance of equanimity in our outlook; to be able to observe our experience without getting tripwired into reactions about it either way; to stay in our centre amidst extremities. I still haven't found this level of composure in my life. However, I have got as far as being able consciously to 'witness' the majority of my feelings and experiences while they are happening, and this is a helpful mindfulness technique.

OBSERVATION WITHOUT JUDGEMENT

The ever-present inner witness that we can learn to connect with in meditation is like the part of us that has no agenda. It just watches without judging and notices what is going on without getting attached to a story around it. We can experience both the witnessing and the reactive sides of ourselves simultaneously, but the length of our fuse will probably dictate which one we act on. The more we practise mindfulness, the more familiar we become with the act of consciously watching whatever arises. This might give the impression that we also become serene and peaceful, but in reality I think we just become more aware and able to pause for breath before responding to people and situations.

Watching without judgement, rather than reacting, is a theme that I constantly work and struggle with as a parent, finding myself unable 'to see the wood for the trees' in my efforts at times. But trying is at least one step in the right direction. And my motivation to try comes from a real feeling of compassion for my children and a dedication to their happiness, as is the case for most parents. This is what we need to draw on during those fleeting windows of awareness when our children's wills conflict with our own. We need to embrace that overarching wish for them to be well and let this work through our words and actions, so that even when we feel agitated or agonized by our offspring, we can still try to find a positive light to view them in.

Like and dislike are inherently human, yet they can also hugely limit the way we handle difficulties. If we can reach just a little bit further into the essence of our compassion by trying to put ourselves in the shoes of our child, we can soften edges and enable kindness and care to flow both outwards to them and inwards to ourselves. If we can be conscious of the stress triggers and patterns which may exacerbate tension for us and practise staying centred at these times, we can navigate more safely through the angst and arguments, the toddler tears and teenage tantrums, and in times of conflict find a middle ground between the extremes.

Humour,
Play and Movement

Mothering children can undoubtedly be a hilarious
pastime for anyone who enjoys a bit of silliness. That
moment when a child unwittingly comes out with
a double entendre, like my four-year-old's innocent
naming of the lead protagonist in our made-up story,
'Fartrick', who later became 'Parktrick' after she realized
that his name suggested he could do tricks with farts.
Or slapstick scenes like a parent cast off balance by a
marauding toddler and sent careering into the mud.
Public places can be glorious grounds for delighting
in our child's embarrassing antics, too, such as the long,
loud and malodorous filling of a nappy on public
transport, or the random exclamations and personal

questions that our children might put to complete strangers, like 'Why is your hair hanging on?' or 'Has he got a baby in his tummy?'

Chances to chuckle are ubiquitous and thank goodness they are, because without them we might find ourselves in despair. Laughter makes us feel great. It releases stress and stimulates the production of our health-building love hormone, oxytocin. Our children, too, are devoted advocates of its medicinal powers; they are drawn towards anything that will charm a laugh out of them. When you are up against the grit of parenting that we all face now and then, see if encouraging a few giggles brings light relief and eases your situation.

CONNECTING TO THE PRESENT MOMENT

Another excellent tactic for setting sail on a brighter trajectory is play. Even adults know the language of play, although we are less likely to use it as often as our juniors. We could be at our wits' end with our offspring, yet by suddenly introducing a game or fantastical adventure into the fray we may find that we can capture our child's imagination and creatively steer our interaction out of the Bermuda Triangle and into the Cape of Good Hope. A young child's world is so creative that real and imagined events can influence each other easily, enabling a free flow of ideas and thoughts to dart between them. This means it is possible to uplift a stormy mood through puppeteering stuffed toys or storytelling, or to help a child focus on an activity with the help of an enthusiastic 'friend', made imaginatively animate. Even an older child can engage with play if they feel unselfconscious, especially out in nature where tree stumps make great hideaways and sticks can become all manner of outdoor equipment.

When we allow things to be fun we cannot help but wake up into the present moment. This kind of spontaneous creativity demands that we keep on our toes and are fully engaged in being 'here and now', co-creating and morphing in and out of theatrical forms.

MOVEMENT AND WELLBEING

A key part of imaginative play involves using our bodies. Physical movement lies at the heart of our self-expression and this in itself can become a therapeutic practice because the endorphins we generate enhance our sense of wellbeing.

Have you ever spent too many fidgety, squabbling hours indoors with your children on a rainy day and, in a bolt of inspiration, decided to put some music on and turn it up? If so, do you remember how your kids responded? Was there an exclamation of 'Yes!' or a jumping up for a chance to choose the next song? And did indoor-rainy-day dances ensue? If so, then it sounds like you cracked the recipe for reconnecting with fun through movement. And if not, then maybe this idea will spur you on. Many of us love to dance from a young age, but are not always encouraged or given the chances to do so, or are told that dance has to be something we learn in a class, and so maybe we lose interest. Perhaps we believe that some of us can dance while others can't.

But the truth is that we can all move. We don't have to be Shakira to shimmy or Rudolf Nureyev to pirouette. Playing and dancing for fun couldn't be more natural for most children. We just need to let it happen freely. When we move our body, we move both our physical and subtle energy systems, which starts a process of detoxification – the body's answer to letting go. And as our physiology releases, often our psycho-emotional baggage can be more ready to shift too. Moving and dancing regularly has the power to uplift us and to hugely improve our health and happiness, and our children can be our guiding gurus here.

Boundaries and
Compromise

Since becoming a mother I have always felt as if I am no longer a single entity but that somehow my children and I have morphed into parts of each other. I carry them inside me wherever I go, like a couple of extra organs, and my life is coloured inextricably by their presence within it. A psychologist might say that this sounds unhealthy, and I sometimes wonder if I am alone in feeling this way. I think it is just a part of the maternal condition, that for at least some of our lives we feel a very strong connection with our children, which will certainly fluctuate and change over the years, finding its own rhythmic way in and around our ongoing parallel lives.

Nevertheless, there may be times when we need to firm up our boundaries with our children, to give clear guidelines and to 'be the parent in the room', so to speak. This can rock the family boat and affect the feeling of closeness we have with them, yet it is necessary and essential at times. While we may hate to curb or disappoint them at one level, circumstances may call for it, to benefit everyone involved, even though we may be momentarily disliked for it. This is a big sting for any parent who loves to be loved. But we also know that what our children need and what they want can be two quite different things.

POWER STRUGGLES

'Yes, I know you want to play on that device and no, you can't play on it right now because you need to get outside into the fresh air' – does that have a familiar ring to your ears? This announcement may become the prelude to a protest, followed by an antagonistic dialogue about why it needs to happen. Food and eating habits can also be the source of endless power struggles between parent and child, to the extent that a family eventually relinquishes whatever rules they may have started out with about what, where and when their children eat, just to avoid this. The desire-driven trait in us human beings does not like being put off course or reined in, and in many instances our children's instinct is just to push back.

THE ART OF COMPROMISE

A traditional technique for reclaiming an object from a baby or toddler is to introduce and engage them with another 'more interesting' object while sneakily removing the former one before they notice. Although this may seem somewhat underhanded, it can also be seen as a compromise made with someone who is not yet of an age to negotiate verbally. Either way, our infant remains serene because they have their object, or an even better one, and everyone is happy.

When it comes to negotiating restrictions with an older child, the tactics of compromise can also come into their own. If we devise an outcome that meets a need for both parent and child, each can feel that their wants have been acknowledged and to some extent fulfilled, even if they have had to give up something else in the process. This does not have to pan out as, 'If you do this for me, I will give this to you', or 'out-and-out bribery' as we refer to it in my household. It can actually be far more positive and creative, whereby there is a mutual recognition of our needs and aims, resulting in a shared understanding and search for ways of getting needs met.

ALLOWING SPACE TO GROW

As our children grow up and become increasingly more independent, we start having to navigate the principle of taking personal space for ourselves, and allowing personal space for them, so that we can each of us grow in our own ways. Many families subscribe to this methodology, but it can also activate anxieties around feelings such as rejection, loss of connection or control, and worry about where a child or teenager is and what they might be doing. Sometimes trying to fortify our boundaries with a teenage child is like adding fuel to the fire of autonomy raging within them, and we can make ourselves outcasts to their world.

Here we can cultivate awareness around our relationship to caretaking, noticing where we feel the urge to control and why. We can explore our anxieties and concerns, and ask ourselves what they are founded on. If our unquestionable love is always at the core of whatever we are feeling about our teenager, then by communicating this before casting reasonable limitations onto their social agenda, we will probably have succeeded in some way just by connecting from the heart first. Our love for them is so important, and they will feel this, but both freedom and boundaries are also healthy aspects of loving.

Creativity

Creativity is a human trait and it is also synonymous with female physiology. We have the fascinating potential to gestate and birth new life. But whether we become mothers or not, this innate creative ability can find parallel expression in our lives, in whatever direction we take it.

Throughout the ages, even during eras when we were prohibited from training and contributing in various fields as professionals in our own right, women have poured their creativity into many forms, from culture to culture across the world. Textiles, medicine, dance, art, science, writing, fashion, politics, history, sport, education, music, theatre, business, benevolence, spirituality, fine cuisine, design and nature-knowledge; you name it, we have done it or used it to give form to the creative fire within us.

CREATIVITY AS NURTURER

Keeping our creativity alive is one way of staying awake to life. It can be deeply fulfilling to express our unique gift, or contribute our personal note to a collaborative creation. Creativity opens our inner vision as well as our actual eyes, enabling us to develop and to refine ideas and images, to consider our experiments and reflect on our creative acts. It can also challenge our abilities, catalyse self-doubt and dare us to surpass our predefined limits. But one thing is for sure, if we nurture it, it will nurture us.

As spare time shrinks in the early years of parenting, so our creative energies get channelled into the more pressing task of shepherding our little ones. For highly creative souls this phase can feel like we are fasting from the food we need to thrive, and we may want to reach out for support with childcare in order to satiate that hunger to be doing or making again. For some it may be that motherhood itself presents an endlessly inspiring project of childrearing, overflowing with opportunities for innovation and artistry. For many of us, however, the impulse dwelling within us to craft, initiate or pioneer may be temporarily forgotten as it is subsumed into the oftentimes chaotic, all-hands-on-deck experience of being with small children. And this can be dispiriting at times.

FEEL THE FEAR AND DO IT ANYWAY

If, or when, we cannot integrate our creative spark into the day to day of family life, and we are unable to make time for it outside of those perimeters, we may start to notice an emptiness dawning inside that is hard to name. Perhaps an emotional low or a soul-sense of being lost. It may show up as an unhealthy addiction to social media, sugary foods or some other quick fix, or in an entirely different way. But if we can get quiet enough to pick up on the underlying message, we may hear that our inner wellspring of creativity has been damned up and yearns to be set free.

Finding, then, a channel for this energy to flow into is an essential next step and it requires our own generous permission to make it reality. So, if we really want to take up an instrument or learn how to make clothes, we may need to bust the inner voice that tells us we can't, for whatever reason, or maintains that there is no point, or any other excuse it is ready to put forward. We need to raise ardent opposition to this voice, to feel the fear and just do it anyway.

Bringing our awareness to what we experience in the process can also be revealing. Good or even liberating feelings reaffirm our choice to go ahead and try. Fear of failure or emotional discomfort at the start could also lead to us having a greater sense of achievement in the longer term if we keep going. Focusing on the breath can help us go through inner thresholds like these with increased calm.

A SHARED REWARD

Even getting this far in the pursuit of our creative exploits can take courage but if we acknowledge the joy we receive from doing what we love, it will start to seem more like a necessity than an indulgence. Giving ourselves more chances to access our creative side and to feast on soul food affords us greater abundance as parents, too. We can't help but bring more of our whole selves into our families by sharing some of the riches we have uncovered. Fostering a friendship with our passion to create or 'do' in this way can also inspire our children in ways we couldn't predict. They will always carry the example of our creative engagement with the world as an impetus towards what is possible for themselves too. As mothers, doing what we love and loving what we do has to be the way forward.

Food
and Body

Physiologically, being a mother is inseparable from being a woman, and pregnancy, childbirth, breastfeeding and intensive baby-care can all make their marks on a woman's body like no other course of events. We transform through this process, becoming new and different women with new and different bodies – ordinary yet miraculous bodies that now bear witness, like a trophy, to the gift of life we have presented to the world. Some women celebrate their newfound maternal physique and hold themselves with pride, but many of us feel we have lost some of the aura of beauty we previously had, simply because we now have stretch marks, a looseness of skin, or a thicker silhouette.

TURN THE MIRROR INWARDS

In this modern world of mirrors, where our gaze is so focused on the external, the way we look can take the lead in our judgements of each other. Feeling attractive is at a premium, and feeling unattractive can be significantly damaging to our sense of self-worth. The statistics around our destructive preoccupation with weight gain are worryingly high for females of all ages, from as young as early childhood to well beyond the menopause. We put a lot of energy into thoughts and fears about how we look, how we feel about our bodies and how we might try to make them 'better'. In this era of the 'liberated' woman, many of us may find that we are ruling ourselves with an iron rod and chaining our bodies to demands for improvements on the beauty front.

As a woman who, when I was younger, suffered from food-control issues, huge self-consciousness and insecurity about my looks, I understand how deeply the seed of dissatisfaction and even self-loathing can grow in the female psyche. It can literally shut us down by dampening our life-force energy and reducing our self-respect. Thankfully, I have also experienced the wellspring of self-empowerment that can come from turning the mirror to face the wall and declaring my body a zone of loving acceptance, where self-criticism is replaced with gratitude and appreciation for the amazing physical form I inhabit. This is a profoundly important dimension to women's liberation. It has taken many years of mindful awareness and self-listening for me to recognize the thoughts and moments in which compassion has been lacking, to acknowledge these and find the self-kindness needed to heal them.

When we examine our relationship with food we will commonly find telltale indications of how we habitually treat our body and how we speak to ourselves at a less conscious level. Eating certain foods can summon feelings of shame and regret and kindle new searches for weight-loss regimes. We might replace self-kindness with food and use it to comfort us, or we might punish ourselves inwardly for eating the 'wrong' food and praise ourselves for sticking to the 'right' diet. Bringing your awareness to the inner monologue that exists around what you eat, and how you look, might help you shed more light on this dynamic.

When we strip away to the bare bones behind these messages what we often find is a pattern of self-control that seeks to determine what makes us lovable or unlovable, desirable or undesirable, in the eyes of others. Where self-criticism features large for someone, there can usually be found a low-level lack of self-belief or a sense of unworthiness that goes beyond any physical attribution. Rather it has been projected from the mind onto the body like an image onto photographic paper.

COURAGE AND COMPASSION

Becoming conscious of this can help us to initiate and sustain change, but if we truly want to reclaim our personal freedom from self-limiting convictions and beliefs, there are two other equally important skills we need to cultivate, and these are courage and self-love.

It can take a lot of courage and dedication to develop a compassionate relationship with ourselves. I know this from experience; it is hard work to stand up consistently to the inner critic, but the rewards are abundant.

As mothers, the impetus to feed our children is instinctual and comes from a place of loving care. How would it be for us to explore feeding ourselves in this way too? Ensuring that we meet our own needs when we are hungry and thirsty; tanking up on the kind of sustenance that nourishes and grants us good health? Food is energy and vitality and we can use it wisely to gain more of these qualities. Mothering the mother is not always easy to do when our children also need us to be there for them, but in order to approach our complex role with resilience, it helps if we can learn how to cherish ourselves. We can then, by example, teach our children how to love themselves too.

Delegation and
Appreciation

Have you ever walked into a room strewn with clothes, toys and books, and found yourself saying, 'Why is it always me who has to deal with this?' Perhaps a few years down the line your response might become, 'OK, why haven't the kids dealt with this?' When parenting, there is a natural progression from 'I have to do this' to 'we have to do this', as we learn to delegate fairly and share responsibilities with our children. This forms healthy and necessary habits within a family, and whether our kids like it or not, they need to get used to helping out.

Even so, it can be difficult at times for us to witness the unquestioned expectations that others have of us or to see how effortlessly our offerings can be received without so much as a thank you. We mothers and fathers are so loved and needed and yet our role is so frequently unappreciated and even unnoticed.

LESSONS FOR LIFE

Although it is a completely normal scenario for a child to take for granted a caregiver who has always been there for them, the truth is that in order to help our offspring develop a sense of mindful appreciation for what they have in their lives, we need to introduce them to the practice of recognizing and thanking the efforts of others to support them. If you find yourself wincing at the thoughtless complaint your child bestows upon the meal you have just lovingly prepared for them, then this is probably the moment to draw their attention to those two powerful concepts, 'recognition' and 'thanksgiving', and encourage them to put both into practice. Likewise when they notice your endeavours, show that recognition flows both ways by being sure to welcome their appreciation.

Our children will never have a real understanding about what a parent gives until they become parents themselves. However, when they are faced with the task of cooking a meal or cleaning up after one, their eyes cannot help but be opened to the effort that is involved. This is great life experience, and it engages them with the cycle of daily family events through participating rather than simply being served. Even little ones can feel a sense of empowerment through being 'in charge' of some aspect of domestic life. From the age of three I proudly stood on my milk crate by the kitchen counter and assembled my sandwiches for school every day, and at some level the belief I created while doing so was that 'I am capable'. This is such a positive message to send our children into the world with.

By giving everyone a significant role to play in the general running of things at home, we also do our children the service of showing them how to think beyond the box of 'me' and to become more aware of contributing to the group. This focus on taking wider responsibility for the whole is essential for young people, enabling them to build self-esteem and purpose in life. And through recognizing their own positive impact they can find greater self-appreciation and motivation to continue their efforts, building this into a valuable aspect of their identity as future adults.

A MATTER OF BALANCE

By contrast, the effects of not entrusting daily jobs to one's brood can lead to feelings of martyrdom and resentment for parents. And the meaning our children might make of us wielding these attitudes is that they themselves are not capable. No one wins in this situation and the mutual accumulation of negative feelings can lead to a deterioration in our relationship overall. If either our children, or we ourselves, are resistant to the division of chores in our family, then we may need to openly examine why this is and to configure a strategy in which everyone gets their needs relatively well met. If a child does not understand the benefits of their helping, for both themselves and others, it can be useful to explore this with them in a new light, underlining how important it is to have a special job.

Failing this, some negotiation around rewards may reinforce your message. Call it bribery if you must, or a cultivation of willingness, but in all cases, parenting children who are able to lend us a hand will unfailingly make us more enthusiastic in our provision for them, too. And though our children give to us in so many other ways, from a cuddle to a few kind words that can make our day, being able to experience the cyclic flow of energy found in giving and receiving at a practical level, can be just the right kind of refreshment needed to revive a tired and weary mother.

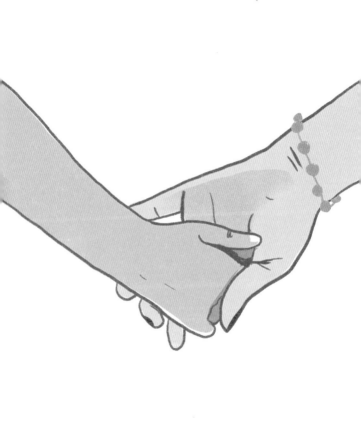

Conflict and
Communication

In all familial settings our edges will come up against
each other at times and it is very likely that our
communication skills will be severely challenged when
the sparks fly. If there are any moments when we will
be less attracted to using mindful speech, and actually
most in need of it, it's these ones. So this is a daring
arena to bring the tools of listening and expressing
ourselves in a reflective way.

Although conflict is a natural aspect of intimacy,
sometimes yelling at each other can hurt a lot and the
hurt can go deep, leaving us in a field of mistrust and
misunderstanding, where our sense of connection with
each other is weakened. This is impetus enough to try

and introduce better ways of addressing volatile issues or patterns between parental partners, or between parents and children, but to do this we need to become really truthful with ourselves.

HONESTY WITHOUT BLAME

Here we can draw on the art of mindful observation of the thoughts and emotions that rise up within us when we are triggered. Once identified, we can follow these responses to their source, where our deeper needs and vulnerabilities lie. When we find these connections it starts to make sense that conflict can be fuelled by the activation of our emotional wounds, evoking in us feelings of threat or rejection and making us feel unloved, blamed or unsafe. When two people are activated in this way, mere words can become daggers, and as we wield them, we may be unaware of our opponent's injuries.

It takes enormous courage and willpower to stand naked in the face of this kind of onslaught, and simply to speak from the hurt part of ourselves, to say, 'I feel hurt', and then to explain why, without blaming. Marshall Rosenberg blazed the trail of this methodology in the 1960s with his programme of NVC, or Non-Violent Communication, which has since become a globally recognized strategy for diffusing tension while yielding greater understanding and empathy. 'Behind every feeling is a need', Rosenberg asserts, and his approach offers a practice that can be used by each participant to state their feelings and needs with non-accusatory language.

THE POWER OF TRUST

What Non-Violent Communication provides is a safe emotional space in which people can express what is really going on for them at a deeper level without feeling that they will be attacked or rejected in doing so. When we have this rare opportunity to pull down some of the defensive walls we have built around our most fragile, wounded parts, it is quite astounding how much compassion can arise naturally between us. Suddenly there is nothing left to protect, as we are able to see our common fears and vulnerabilities reflected by one another's deep honesty. This makes it is easier for us to own them in ourselves and to accept them in others, and it is especially useful during the teenage years when our offspring's worldview may diverge significantly from our own and our patience and empathy with each other will tire. Even so, when each 'adversary' can articulate themselves with care, clarity and authenticity it is possible to establish a common ground of trust, and trust is ultimately the most solid and real way out of conflict. Trust is also needed to forge any kind of meaningful or peaceful future ahead.

ACCEPTANCE AND CURIOSITY

However, for many reasons it may not be possible to use techniques like this to reduce effectively the combative energy we find ourselves coping with when we clash. Perhaps it's not your style to use formalized language to express yourself, or to expect this of those close to you, and it is certainly something that even people who try to practise Non-Violent Communication still tussle with. But if we can at least pause for a breath before responding to the drama, and accept that quarrelling and closeness are bedfellows within a family, it can ultimately make for less friction.

If you, like me, are an emotional person, it may be helpful to find space for a bit of private screaming – into a pillow or out in nature, for example – as this can bring the heat of one's own feelings down to more of a simmer and make the prospect of speaking to our children or partner more manageable. Expressing our emotions safely can also provide us with a curious view into them: what are they about? Where do they come from and what lies beneath them? These questions can keep us in a space of conscious awareness around what we feel and why, which can potentially help us to begin deconstructing the reactive catalysts in us even before they flare up into confrontations.

Teenagers
– Safety and Surrender

The long-standing metaphor of the river whose waters find their way over and around rocks and boulders has been well used to represent the equipoise and resilience we sometimes need to meet life's difficulties. And parenting teenagers is probably going to be the right time to maximize and lean into our capacity to do just that. But in order to do so we may need to change the way we see our growing children, to reframe the judgements and expectations we have of them, and to explore relating with them in a whole new way.

The greatest resource we can draw on as we begin this process is the power of memory: while reflecting on our own personal recollections of what life was like for us on that tenuous cusp between child and adult, we can empathize more readily with our adolescent teens. This stage of parenting can potentially be as challenging as it can be healing, if our own teenage years were difficult. We might remember what we yearned for and what we needed. We may be reminded of all those insecurities and the stark self-consciousness that hung around us, the peer pressure, the desperation to fit in and be liked or, conversely, to stand out and command attention. These are the traits we find in teen-limbo as adulthood beckons. And it is good to be aware that as our children get bigger, and their school workloads heavier, their vulnerabilities can actually feel much more exposed.

On the other hand, these fledgling years also bring a hunger for fun and freedom that could confront us as parents more than we imagined. Our teen's surge towards independence might be expressed through a kind of generalized irritation with being parented at all, yet those underlying teenage insecurities may bring them into a contrary position of both wanting, and not wanting, security from us. Here we see echoes of the toddler years resonating through our child's need for us being coupled with their demand for greater control over their lives, as they find their own sense for self and place in the world. And physiologically, their bodies are undergoing an irreversible revolution, cannons blazing, and the hormones in command will be inconveniently calling out riotous battle cries periodically.

GOING WITH WHAT WORKS

For a parent in this situation, we can choose to fight our teen or, like the river, to follow a path of least resistance. The notion of surrender here provides us with a choice to go with, rather than against, whatever struggle is present. This may mean yielding control, or giving up on our personal agenda in order to find some common ground with our child. Surrendering can enable us to become receptive and go with what works while abandoning whatever doesn't. It can be likened to 'listening', because as soon as we truly start to listen to any situation, we cease trying to control it. Paying attention in this way also requires our willingness to do so, either from a place of curiosity or compassion, or both. On this trajectory we may, in time, start to uncover an inner strength founded on the wisdom of not 'sweating the small stuff'. We might begin to evaluate everyday scenarios and ask ourselves, 'Is this a life or death situation?', then decide to respond by avoiding drama, knowing that we can choose our battles and sidestep any longer-term deterioration of our relationship.

A SAFE SPACE

But this youthful phase of life also craves initiation, which can involve a shattering of innocence and playing with fire that takes both our child and ourselves way out of our comfort zones. If a potential risk to them is too great, obviously their safety and wellbeing takes priority and we will feel this is worth fighting for.

However, we don't necessarily have to take it on as conflict, because conflict will just add fuel to the flames. On the contrary, if we want to hold any sway over our child's increasing independence, we will somehow need to remain non-judgemental and maintain open channels of communication.

Giving our children the space required for this may be testing, for this space must have the feeling of freedom and privacy from us, and yet be safe enough for them to connect with us. We may need to put our own vulnerabilities on the back shelf in order to be really present for them. Even if they choose not to engage with us, by trusting, loving and staying open to them in this way our presence can create an invisible container for them as they begin to expand out into their own life. In time, if they sense that we are truly there for them and interested in who they are, then gradually they can develop the confidence to enter more fully into their adult selves.

Self-nourishment and
Renewal

The image of the self-sacrificing mother is a traditional
archetype in our culture because it describes the role
that has been modelled from mother to daughter for
the last few millennia. Although today most women
have so much more freedom in so many ways, we may
still struggle to understand or address what we actually
need in order to feel nourished at a deeper level. A
mother is especially vulnerable to this because from her
first baby onwards she becomes used to putting her
children's needs before her own. But when a mother
goes unnourished, the whole family hungers on many
levels. Even if this is not glaringly obvious at first, it
may become so later on.

The socially accepted quick fixes we are used to 'treating' ourselves with – perhaps that much-longed-for glass of wine at the end of the day, cake and coffee in lieu of lunch, a new pair of shoes that we can't really afford but had to get – merely skate across the subject of truly 'giving' to ourselves. There is nothing wrong with them as such, but they are superficial, fleeting 'feel-good' perks. If we confuse them with self-care but use them as such, we will still end up running on empty in the long term. So how can we take more solid steps towards knowing our underlying needs and getting them met?

TAKING TIME TO DO NOTHING

I believe that anything that counteracts the busyness of our lives is going to get some positive results. Mothers are often juggling work, home and family – and that's just the hors d'oeuvres. The to-do lists can seem endless, and quickly filled diaries may leave us asking ourselves, 'Where is there space for me in all of this?' It sounds simplistic, but to pioneer change through relaxation when our lives are moving at full pelt, the practical approach of *taking* a bit of time each day, just to stop and do nothing but rest, is an excellent starting point.

You may notice I have emphasized the word 'taking' here… Some might even use the phrase 'stealing time', because for many mothers the chance of resting for a while in the day seems selfish and impossible and might elicit feelings of guilt. Does guilt arise for you at the thought of doing things for yourself rather than for your family or work? If so, it is worth becoming curious about those feelings and gently asking the question, why wouldn't you want to be generous towards yourself, considering all you do for others?

NURTURING THE NURTURER

Making space for oneself to explore quietude, presence and 'refuge' from the busy world is an act of self-kindness that can and does nurture us. It is unusual in this fast-paced era for us to give precedence to such a thing. We might imagine it to be a waste of time. But if we look beyond this and trust in the wisdom of gifting ourselves a day in solitude or perhaps a weekend away or on retreat, we may encounter a wealth of soulful riches within us. Given the chance to stop, we may also discover our own exhaustion and realize that all we want to do is sleep. Through resting we can start to replenish our reserves of strength and through reflection we can rekindle our sense of self, asking ourselves, 'what do I need?' and acting on this.

RENOVATION AND RENEWAL

There is a saying that goes, 'When our hands are full, they cannot receive. Learn how to let go.' Stopping in our tracks can also reveal to us quite how full to the brim we are, and letting go is another way in which we can receive nourishment. As mothers, for many years we literally cradle and carry our children, and even when they are walking on their own two feet we still keep their wellbeing in our hearts and minds. There might be times when we get so used to this aspect of 'holding' our children, both practically and emotionally, that we forget the need to 'recycle' our own energy, to empty out our worries and woes and to start over again. Imagine living in a home that we never cleaned or cleared out – how would it feel? Yet there may be times when we recognize that we are carrying around metaphorical 'bags of trash', old stories, habits, ideas and emotions that no longer serve us.

The more we consciously listen to our hearts and minds, the more we can begin to detect 'self-talk' – our internal thoughts – that may require renovation too. We might start to notice destructive thought patterns and beliefs that make us feel trapped. But if we can tune our inner ear to the key of self-kindness, we may feel inspired to experience more care for ourselves, and this can become a powerful vehicle for transformation.

Mother Nature,
Mother Nurture

Being in nature with the family will always bring a different quality to the way we are together. Children tend to relax more outdoors, and the sense of adventure and team building we can experience on a camping trip or a rugged day out often uncovers surprising new features in a child's burgeoning personality. The sun does not have to be shining; on the contrary, if we are well prepared, a bit of adversity in weather conditions can do more to reveal our strength of character and deliver a sense of achievement and bonding as we overcome difficulties. And, significantly, it can bring us into the fore of our mindful awareness through waking up our sense faculties and our survivalist need to be present.

THE ART OF OBSERVATION

We may arrive somewhere in nature, tumbling out from our car with the radio on, holding onto our strands of conversation and plans for the day, and it may take us a while to acclimatize to where we are. We may be half a mile or so down the trail before we consciously start to notice the colours of the sky, the scents in the air or the kinds of plants, mosses or lichens lining our path. But when we do stop to give our attention to these things, it is as if the world opens up to intensify our perception of them. Earth colours and tree shapes meet our eyes more boldly. Sounds sharpen and define themselves clearly to ears that listen intently. Temperatures sink into our skin as we feel the touch of warm and cool breezes.

If your children don't seem to click automatically with this notion of becoming sensitive to their environment through the instrument of their senses, try asking them simple questions such as, 'What sounds can you hear?' and see if they can delve through layer upon layer of sounds into the distance. Or, 'What are the nearest and furthest things that you can see?', or 'Can you smell the air?' It might interest them to know that many traditional peoples and also animals can smell and sense weather changes in the air, like rain, snow and warmth, days before they show up locally.

Enquiring into the environment like this is a good way to attune to where we are, shifting our attention from the rigours of our own mind's preoccupations, to that of the intriguing yet 'ordinary' natural surroundings we find ourselves in. As we shift into observation mode our train of thought may quieten, but we will need to gather some degree of inner calm in order to begin listening at all.

LEARNING TO BE QUIET

If your family tends to talk a lot, you might find it interesting to call for silent slots in the day, say five to fifteen minutes, where no one speaks. This tends to work well outside, where everyone can wander off and 'be' in their own space more. For very busy children a silent activity might work best, either making drawings or lists of all the phenomena they notice during their non-verbal time slot. It can be fascinating to note what your child makes of these encounters with quietude. Parents and children can be mutually inspired by each other's hushed study of their world.

NATURE AS RESTORER

Alternatively, being out and about on our own can grant us the prospect of having quiet time without having to ask for it. I find that my solo walks in the woods help me to drop into a more meditative state of connection with the land that holds me. As a busy mother, carving out this time and space to absorb nature and to feel supported by it, is something that restores me. I am constantly learning from these experiences, from sitting still and observing and listening, from moving through the landscape, from glimpsing into the habits of insects, birds and animals, and from feeling my feet on the earth.

As we soak up the seasons, we are offered the opportunity to witness a perpetual progression taking place: the cycle of birth, death and rebirth that is reflected to us endlessly in the natural world, month after month, year after year. Although we almost take this perennial pattern for granted, it is an utterly key element of life, and it reminds us that creation, and re-creation, is the primary guiding principle on this planet. The organic matter that germinates, grows and decays back into the earth, also nourishes it. Taking note of nature's recycling plan can help us as mothers to recognize that what we 'birth' into the world can nourish us too, if we choose to receive it.

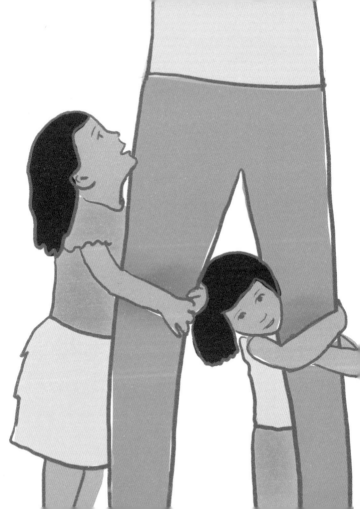

Celebration and Presence

You are a mother. You are raising, or have raised, another human being to adulthood. Have you ever paused to fully acknowledge yourself for this monumental task? It may seem so ordinary, so mundane an undertaking, yet it requires dedication beyond anything we may have previously known in our lives. And this deserves our recognition, because in today's culture, except on Mother's Day, it may go unnoticed by others.

THE GIFT OF PRAISE

Self-celebration might sound like a big ego trip, but in reality it is a way of affirming all our efforts and gifts that we put to use in serving our children. This could just be stopping every once in a while to admire our work, or saying 'Well done!' to ourselves when we succeed in some way. It might feel a bit strange doing this. Do I really need to congratulate myself, you might ask. Am I nuts? But it is a strategy that can help us to build the benevolent ability to celebrate and feel pride, whether for ourselves or for others. When we can begin to celebrate the simple things as well as the big events in our lives, we allow for the small joys to contribute more to our general sense of fulfilment.

If you would like to adopt this way of thinking into the way you tackle daily life, it can be helpful to just observe or even write down some of the characteristics you appreciate about yourself, your personal strengths, your achievements and breakthroughs (however small), your courage to face challenges. Take note of when you feel joyful or generous and think about the ways in which you drink in the riches of your life. Then use this reflective space to honour the amazing and unique woman and mother that you are.

Celebration is a magnificent attitude to bring into family life, too, where there are so many avenues to explore honouring each other. From a baby starting to sleep through the night, to a child overcoming a fear, or a teenager making new friends or achieving something they are passionate about, the possibilities are endless. No one needs to open a bottle of fizz; it could just be a collective, heartfelt 'YAAAYYY!' to mark the occasion.

SHARED MOMENTS

But celebration is not just about developing a positive, affirming attitude within our families. It is also way of calling ourselves into this activity, this feeling and witnessing this moment. As we experience what is being honoured, we become more aware and fully present. Clear glimpses into our own lives such as this provide soul-snapshots that we will remember. And these warm, shared moments give rise to stronger bonds between parents, children and siblings. In schools where celebration has been modelled as an integral part of how pupils' progress is monitored, we find examples of children celebrating each other. It is so heartening to see this current wisdom that is encouraging children to see each other's gifts. If we can continue to educate our young with this astute generosity and care, we will be impressing it into their hearts and thereby ensuring it for their children too.

ALL THAT REMAINS IS NOW

Although it might seem sad or pessimistic to view our lives through a time-bound tunnel, it can also lead us to profound insight if we accept that within fifty years we may not be here, and that every chance we have to celebrate with our children is one to be grasped with both hands in delight. To live one's life with an awareness of its temporal nature, is to live truly. This is a significant theme in Buddhism, which teaches that since the past no longer exists, and the future does not yet exist, all that remains is now. As we try to grasp this concept, our human wills may try to pull us towards finding solidity. Understandably, we might yearn for a reliable foundation on which to base ourselves and we may fight against life's fickle tides.

But in the midst of this bid to maintain the status quo we may feel an equal measure of relief that the monotony of daily repetition is broken up, that we don't know what the weather will be tomorrow and that our inner compass responds to the magnetism of change. The predictable features in our lives will always be set against the backdrop of transformation, unpredictability and the random wilds of our sentient landscape. By cultivating compassion for all of us who ride these waves, we can open our hearts more fully to being here in life. We can learn to celebrate all that we are, have, know and love because . . . this is it!

The
Motherlines

We are the women who have descended from many lines of mothers before us, from ancestral mothers who have grown and lived within their limitations of time and place. And in most ways we are probably freer and more empowered than any of our female predecessors. Among many of the positive changes that have taken place for women with the passing of time is the shift in attitudes towards how we parent our children.

Scanning over recent social history it is easy to find examples of hard-hearted and controlling attitudes that have been encouraged towards children. Ingrained fears of 'spoiling' our young ones and even babies with too much affection took root in past centuries, making the world a colder place for countless children. The resurgence of more compassionate, humanistic ideals only occurred relatively recently in the West, initially with Dr. Spock in the 1940s and later Jean Liedloff, followed by William and Martha Sears in the 1980s, who all helped to reintroduce a more empathetic and instinctual approach to childrearing.

Historically, there is a striking parallel between women being culturally suppressed and affection being withheld from children With the gradual emancipation of women has come the social development of more caring and humane ways of relating to our offspring. And in truth it seems staggeringly clear that our maternal urge to soothe, comfort and love our little ones was somehow dammed up by those tough societal structures of eras gone by. When we look at how far we have come, from this viewpoint, it contextualizes the comparative freedom that we now have to raise our children as beloved and loving people. Technology aside, I see this as one of the greatest advancements of our age.

UNCONSCIOUS PARENTING

Yet to paint a rainbow, it helps if we have learnt the full spectrum of colours. So how can we give to our children what we ourselves perhaps did not receive when we were young? And how can we become more aware at those times when we display parenting traits that we wish our parents had not passed to us? As with so much of our activity, our mothering will often happen unconsciously whether we like it or not. We will react to things in the moment and then later perhaps wonder why we responded in that way, and sometimes we may have insights about why it happened.

If we look deeply into our own childhood we will often find the answers to subtleties in our relationships with our children that reflect our parent's attitudes to us. We cannot help but be conditioned by the powers at play within our families as we grew up. It goes with the territory. To some extent we bring the influences of our mothers and fathers, our grandmothers and grandfathers, and so on, down through the lines as we parent.

SELF-ENQUIRY AND HEALING

This is not always an easy place from which to nurture the family we make, especially if there has been tension or trauma in our past. We may find sticking points with our children that never seem to get easier, or encounter the unhealed areas in ourselves highlighted by being a parent. Attending to these sensitivities might take a lifetime's effort and could require some outside help, but the going will undoubtedly get easier if we can call on the wisdom of mindfulness practice to start becoming more conscious. This can take the form of breath and body awareness to begin with, at the very moment we find ourselves getting stuck into that well-worn rut or pattern.

However, we can also work with self-enquiry during meditation to go a little further down the route of where a particular feeling originates. When did we first feel it? Who were we with and what was happening? As we begin to uncover the tracks of our thoughts and feelings, tracing them through our autobiography, the story of our vulnerabilities and habits may seem clearer. And the more consciously we know these stories, the more likely it is that we will be able to respond with compassion, which, from the discerning heart of a mother, is going to be a good outcome.

The relationship dynamic a mother has with her children is set to make each one grow and perhaps ultimately to bring healing to us all. Would we be the same women were it not for each of our children? I think not. They endlessly show up the places in which we are yet to become whole and inspire us to be so. How would it feel to embrace the relationship you have with them as one in which the teaching and learning keeps flowing in all directions? I wonder what our foremothers would make of that?

The Journey
Onwards

The Dalai Lama, who declares himself a feminist, has stated that, 'The world will be saved by the Western woman'. He communicates the message that mothers in particular have an immensely important role to play in building happy generations of people, because our nurture and affection makes such a difference to the deep self-esteem and confidence our children feel. Concern about the wellbeing of our descendants, both now and in the future, is a theme that is entwined with motherhood. We are configured biologically and instinctually to protect and care for others, not just our own kin. And though we may have been stereotyped and funnelled into caregiver roles since time immemorial, there is an undeniable, innate source of compassion among us, and I believe that it will continue to grow into global movements for change.

A POISONED LEGACY

In recent centuries, care for the welfare of human beings has been sidelined in favour of the productivity and advancement of the industrial age. Greed and materialism have flourished, while Mother Earth – who provides for us all – has been treated as a commodity: her soil drained of nutrients and toxified by the overuse of chemical pesticides and fertilizers; her waters and atmosphere polluted; her diverse species both threatened and made extinct. If, as the UN announced in 2018, all we have left are sixty more harvests from the depleted farmlands that make up around a third of the land on Earth, then what in all honesty will we mothers have to hand down to our children and grandchildren? Fresh food, clean air and water are our greatest priorities for health and life. They cannot be substituted for anything else.

THE TURNING OF TIDES

Becoming increasingly aware of this critical situation may call us to take action. When we engage with mindful awareness as a tool for life, it cannot be limited entirely to ourselves and our personal conditions. Intrinsically, a mindful outlook encompasses all that is around us by acknowledging that we are all part of life's web. When we see areas of this web being hurt it is a bit like watching someone else's child being bullied. It may not be happening to our child, but we know that it is not okay and we want to protect them from harm. Sometimes there is nothing else to do but speak out against injustice, to make waves and forge new pathways based on the wisdom of truth, kindness and respect.

This 'turning of tides' is coded into the blueprint of mythological stories ranging from ancient legends to Disney movies. It is the hero or heroine's journey of transformation that leads us to the ritual 'happy every after' ending, which brings resolution. But right now we are just at the beginning of our epic environmental saga, and perhaps we are wondering if we can really step up into those heroine's shoes when we have our children to care for and such full lives of our own. The question is, do we have a choice? When the world is held in this fragile balance, being destroyed at the rate it is now, our options are slim.

THE WORLD IN OUR HANDS

I believe that the dedication we mothers have for our own families can became a broader commitment to preserving the future of life on this planet. If each of us takes our focus out a little wider to include a political, humanitarian or conservation issue, together our voices can be so much louder. Powerful leaders need to know that we care, and we can use our maternal influence to demonstrate this through taking action in many ways. In our age of commerce, leadership also sits among multi-million-dollar corporate companies who own the multitudes of individual products lining the shelves of our supermarkets and shops. By finding out more about these companies and researching who owns which brands, we can vote with our personal finances to determine who rises and falls in the global marketplace, based on ethical grounds.

All that is needed is for us to look behind the scenes and find out more about the long-term health and ecological impacts created by so many industries. From industrial farming to the shocking production and widespread use of palm oil, evidence of environmental destruction is rife. The production of indigo denim, the shipping industry and the excessive and indiscriminate use of plastic are threatening our sea life with wave after wave of pollution. Filling the fuel tank is deadening our air and causing respiratory illnesses in children. By taking a consumer's stand against these and other ecological issues we can choose another way. As mothers we are able to achieve so much, and can do so globally if we direct our concerns outwards to the Earth as a whole, for the benefit of our families, for all beings now and for the generations to come.

ACKNOWLEDGEMENTS

Heartfelt thanks to my own mother, to the mothers who have contributed in some way to the words on these pages and to all those who join me at themotherspace.com to find more peace and depth on this amazing motherhood journey.

Deep gratitude to my family, Robin, Anoushka and Orlando for their love, acceptance and humour as I wrote this book . . . our life experience together is woven into it all.